THE ART OF
WESTERN AFRICA

Sculpture and Tribal Masks

x

INTRODUCTION BY

WILLIAM FAGG

A MENTOR-UNESCO ART BOOK

PUBLISHED BY
THE NEW AMERICAN LIBRARY, NEW YORK AND TORONTO
BY ARRANGEMENT WITH UNESCO

MENTOR TRADEMARK REG. U. S. PAT. OFF. AND FOREIGN COUNTRIES
REGISTERED TRADEMARK—MARCA REGISTRADA

MENTOR-UNESCO ART BOOKS ARE PUBLISHED IN THE UNITED STATES BY
THE NEW AMERICAN LIBRARY, INC.,
1301 AVENUE OF THE AMERICAS, NEW YORK, NEW YORK 10019,
IN CANADA BY THE NEW AMERICAN LIBRARY OF CANADA LIMITED,
295 KING STREET EAST, TORONTO 2, ONTARIO
PRINTED IN ITALY BY AMILCARE PIZZI S.P.A. MILANO

In our imaginary journey to survey the styles of African sculpture, we find ourselves following quite naturally the path of the first European discoverers sailing from Portugal in the fifteenth century. As we shall see, these explorers were by no means indifferent to the native art which they found there in full flower. Our own introduction to it, soon after we round Cape Verde, is no gradual or gentle one, for the very first cluster of art-producing tribes—in Portuguese Guinea and along the neighbouring coast of the Republic of Guinea—is dominated artistically by what is surely the most powerful and uncompromising of all African images: the great *nimba* mask of the Baga (see Fagg, *Tribes and forms in African art*, plate 4). The great cantilevered head of this mask expresses in the most dramatic way those ideas of increase which are central to the African religions, and which were forgotten by Europe when the Roman legions brought civilization and detribalization from the south.

Other tribes of this cluster—the Bijugo, the Nalu and the Landuman, all likewise speaking languages of the West Atlantic group—have their own characteristic masks and figures (op. cit., plates 1-3). In the present volume they are represented by a slighter, more charming example of Baga art (Plate 1), which illustrates almost as well as the *nimba* masks the preoccupation of the Baga artists with the interpretation through sculptures of the idea of increase. This is a dance headdress representing a hornbill, the strong curve of whose beak provides the theme of the whole composition.

Thus we learn at the outset of our survey that—like

5

Athena, born fully armed from the head of Zeus—African sculpture, occupying its vast region of West and Central Africa, does not peter out in a half-world or twilight zone of inferior or isolated creativity at its geographical edges, but meets us full-blown approximately at the border between Senegal, where no representational sculpture is known, and Portuguese Guinea. So it is elsewhere along the boundaries of the great art area of Africa which comprises the vast basins of the Niger and Congo rivers. (If, on the other hand, we look at African sculpture from the historical rather than from the geographical angle, we do find that it ends, in Eliot's well-known words, " not with a bang but a whimper ".)

We cannot tell what the Portuguese thought of the *nimba* masks of the Baga; but we do know that they were much interested in a related style which was then being practised by the Sherbro or Bulom tribe of Sierra Leone, for a large number (probably at least seventy-five) of finely carved ivory salt-cellars and other objects made during the sixteenth century by African carvers to Portuguese commissions have come to light over the years among the royal and noble houses of Europe. These are of great artistic interest as early—and remarkably successful—examples of fusion of European and African artistic ideas, and indeed, the manner in which exotic African ornament was grafted on to the Renaissance forms of these utensils for the tables of those who were also the great patrons of European art of the time may conceivably have played some part in the rise of the Baroque soon afterwards. It can easily be demonstrated that the style of these Afro-Portuguese ivories (excluding, for this purpose, a smaller number carved by Benin artists) and that of the ancient soapstone figures (*nomoli*) of Sierra Leone are one and the same. As a result we are able both to place the ivories and to date the *nomoli*.

Until about 1540 (as we know from Portuguese records) the Sherbro and Kisi cultures stretched unbroken from the Atlantic to the interior borders of Sierra Leone and far into what is still the Kisi country of Guinea. This was one of only three or four tribal complexes in Africa that produced a substantial art in stone (the others being the Yoruba and Ekoi peoples of Nigeria and the Bakongo peoples of the Congo mouth). The Sherbro and Kisi sculptors, though sharing the same subject-matter (chiefly standing and squatting human figures from 10 to 30 cm in height) and material, had evolved distinguishable styles. The Kisi favoured a rather rigidly vertical conception of the figure (comparable to " pole sculpture "), whereas the Sherbro (in keeping with the greater artistic exuberance of the peoples of the Guinea Coast) achieved a greater plastic freedom, and indeed exploited it more thoroughly than any African artists outside the Grasslands of Cameroon. This dual-style complex was rudely severed about 1540 when the attacks of the Mande-speaking Mende drove an enormous wedge between Sherbro and Kisi, and effectively fossilized for us most of their art. The piece shown in Plate 2, said to have been dug up in what is now Temne country, may be regarded as transitional, though with strong Kisi leanings in the form of the head and in the smaller figures grouped under the hands.

East and north-east Liberia, the western Ivory Coast and the neighbouring parts of the interior of Guinea—like the Grasslands of Cameroon and the Ogowe River area of southern Gabon—form a region in which the tribal distribution of art styles remains far from well defined. This is possibly because these three areas can almost be regarded as living laboratories of stylistic change, of fission and fusion of tribal cultures, of assimilation and differentiation of styles, so that only a large fieldwork enterprise, concentrated on this problem alone, is likely to bring order out of the apparent chaos. In the Dan-Ngere tribal complex, the sculpture of a dozen tribes is virtually confined to a single art form, the frontal mask. Moreover, to an extent paralleled in Africa only in the Bwami society of the Balega in the eastern Congo, artistic activity (as indeed most other activities) has been taken over in these tribes by the men's society, the famous *Poro*. The success of this pervasive institution in establishing its control among many other tribes in Sierra Leone, Liberia, Guinea and the Ivory Coast suggests that it is indeed the unifying agent in the field of art. It seems likely that with the help of the *Poro* several variant styles or substyles have been propagated in a complicated pattern among the Dan-Ngere tribes, and that a gradual process of assimilation has been going on there for generations or centuries past. Be that as it may, a remarkable variety of sculptural forms stems from the simple subject-matter of Dan-Ngere masks. Two groups predominate: one, of which Plate 4 is an excellent example, characteristically represents the human face in a rather restrained and naturalistic though subtly simplified way, and is especially associated with the Dan tribe; in the other, which we may call the Ngere mode (see Plate 3, a work from the Gio of Liberia), the human features are strongly stylized, animalized and distorted in expressionist images of power and violence.

Plates 5 and 6 represent examples of Akan art. The group of peoples on the central Guinea Coast who speak the closely related Akan cluster of languages are unusual in several important respects, all of which have a bearing on their art. First, unlike the tribes which we have already examined, they are peoples of the savannah rather than of the forest, and for many centuries have been open, as no other coastal tribes except their Dahomeyan neighbours, to cultural influences coming through the restless Sudan from the Near East. Secondly, they provide the first instance of great kingdoms and empires established and bolstered by military power, in which sheer size and the necessity of administrative elaboration elevate, as it were, the life of the court into a distinct, though related, super-culture; traditional stories tell us that among the Ashanti (as also at Benin) new forms of religion were sometimes introduced for political ends, showing that the state and the divine kingship had become an end in themselves. The third unusual element, which combined the effects of the other two, is again ecological—the land of the Akan (and more particularly of the Ashanti) happens to contain one of the world's richest goldfields.

One more historical fact must be noted before we examine the nature of Akan art itself: we know from traditional stories that the Baule (the second of the two main

Akan tribes) withdrew from the Ashanti and were formed as a separate tribe only about 230 years ago, under their queen Aura Poku, and we must assume that the considerable differences between their arts result from this secession.

Ashanti art is remarkable in that wood sculpture is almost completely unknown—exceptions being the highly stylized dolls (simply a lens-shaped disc supported on a cylinder) carried by young girls, and the wooden rectangular stools which are excellent examples of geometrical, quasi-architectural form. Metalwork predominates, in forms which are mainly decorative (owing to Moslem influences) rather than sculptural. These tendencies were clearly confirmed and emphasized by the discovery of gold, and the fact that gold was reserved for royal use in the jewellery of the court. The human face is treated in a rigidly schematic way, its central feature, the long straight nose joined to semi-circular eyebrows, often suggesting Romanesque arcading.

Baule art, on the other hand, seems to be the product both of fission from the Ashanti matrix and of fusion with the cultures of the Guro and other tribes with whom they mingled to the west. That the essentially schematic lines of the Ashanti style could have been successfully married to the pre-eminently fluid and unbroken curves of Guro wood sculpture is in itself remarkable, and that this could happen in less than two centuries is extraordinary. But the Yaure mask seen in Plate 5 demonstrates its success, even if in our century Baule style has lapsed into sentimental decadence under European commercial influence.

Satellite tribes to the south of the Baule and Ashanti have preserved the pure Akan style chiefly in their terracotta funerary sculpture, for which the Anyi are pre-eminent (Plate 6).

The point at which the hinterland savannah reaches down to the sea, interrupting the forest and offering easy communications with the western Sudan, is a convenient one for us to turn aside to examine the arts of the most important tribes of the sub-desert region. The Senufo, who inhabit a vast area of the northern Ivory Coast,

Upper Volta and southern Mali extending from the nor-thernmost Baule and Ashanti to the Bambara and Dogon, provide a valuable transition both geographically and artistically. They span from south to north the savannah belt which divides the coastal forest from the Sahel, the southern " shore " of the Sahara. And their style of sculp-ture, while never (until recent commercial development) losing its unmistakably strong Senufo character, coexists in the south with the rich exuberance of the Guro-Akan complex and in the north with the severe simplicity, as of wrought iron, which distinguishes the figure sculpture of the western Sudan. They have in fact synthetized the Sudanese and Guinean cultural traditions more success-fully than any other tribe.

Plates 7 and 8 show two variants of one of the most characteristic types of Senufo mask, the *kpelie* or *gpelihe*. Plate 7 represents perhaps the most perfect and complete example known of the classical form of this mask and was collected in the Korhogo district about 1950 (shortly before the general collapse of Senufo style in commercialism and mass-production). The other (Plate 8) was collected in 1889 far to the south-east at Jimini in the Ashanti border-lands of Ghana and is attributed to the Ligbe, a marginal Senufo group now found near Bonduku in the Ivory Coast. Here the characteristic elements of the *kpelie* are present in a simplified form, while the superstructure appears to be influenced by the openwork backs of the *asipem* chairs in which the Ashanti copied Renaissance chairs introduced by the sixteenth-century Portuguese.

The Republic of Mali is the home of some of Africa's finest sculpture, produced chiefly by the Bambara in the west and by the Dogon who inhabit the area of the Ban-diagara Escarpment to the south of Timbuktu. We have noted already a broad difference between the art of the Sudan and that of the Guinea Coast tribes—the former tending towards severely simple, " stripped-down " forms, in contrast with the rich and expansive forms of the coastal peoples. But the distinction is general rather than universal, and there are many exceptions, such as the flamboyant masks of the Bobo of Upper Volta on the one

10

hand, or certain Ijo figures from the Niger Delta, rivalling those of the Dogon in their slender and vertical rigidity, on the other. There are several possible contributory causes for the special quality of most Sudanese sculpture. One is that it represents a kind of accommodation, conscious or unconscious, to the strong geometric tendencies of iconoclastic Islam. Another possible explanation, perhaps too little considered as yet, arises from the fact that in most of the Sudanese tribes the blacksmiths are also the woodcarvers, and form a separate " caste ", preserved through intermarriage, and feared and avoided by the rest of the population, somewhat on the North African model; the fact that their main activity is iron-forging may have excited a strong influence on the design of their woodcarvings, which commonly present an attenuated armature-like quality.

Besides ancestor figures, the Bambara formerly produced a variety of types of masks for several different agricultural and initiatory societies. Of these the most characteristic and famous were the *chi wara* or antelope headdresses used in enactment ceremonies commemorating the birth of agriculture. The example illustrated (Plate 9) is one of the most simplified and " verticalized " of the many abstract forms under which the antelope can be represented, the horns, as usual, being given the greatest emphasis as symbols of growth and spiritual power.

Among the Dogon, the ancestor cult provided the chief *raison d'être* of the sculpture, which is mainly divided between figures and masks. Here as elsewhere, the masks have a comparatively ephemeral, though often deeply moving, character; but many of the ancestor figures—like those of the Oron clan of Calabar, with which they have a peculiar affinity—are among the finest African embodiments in sculpture of the dignity, the *gravitas*, of the ancestors. These figures present an interesting, and rather vexed, problem of art history. They can be readily divided into two main groups: one, of which Plate 10 is a classical example (and at least three other such pieces appear to be from the same hand), is of the rather rigidly ordered type which has been in active ritual use during the present

11

century and seems likely to have developed during the third quarter of the nineteenth. The other, evidently older, is in a freer convention, the composition often deriving its shape from the crooked branch or root from which it was carved. That these are different phases of a single style is proved not only by many correspondences of style and subject-matter but also by the existence of many intermediate pieces. It appears likely that the older works, or some of them, date from the early nineteenth or late eighteenth century and there has as yet been no acceptable evidence to support their attribution to a mythical people, the " Tellem ", said to have been displaced by the Dogon about the fifteenth century. Unfortunately, during the last few years some Dogon have become highly expert forgers of " Tellem " antiquities (often from ancient wood), thus making more difficult the scholar's task of identification.

If we continue through the geographical Sudan into northern Nigeria, we find ourselves before long in the country of the Nok Culture, which was flourishing over a wide area around 280 B.C., as has now been certainly established by the radioactive-carbon method. At that time and probably for several centuries thereafter, the whole central area of what is now Nigeria, today the home of innumerable separate hill tribes, seems to have been occupied by a single people or group of peoples, practising an instantly recognizable form of art, namely terracotta sculpture. Their works are the earliest datable sculptures so far found in negro Africa. These were farming people who had recently emerged into the Iron Age, but were still using more tools of polished stone than of iron (and their culture may therefore be described as siderolithic).

Their sculptural powers at this early time were anything but rudimentary; indeed it can be fairly claimed that they have not been surpassed since. Their technical skill in the handling of clay was also great, for they were able to make almost like-size human figures in terracotta, a feat otherwise attempted in Africa only by the Yoruba of ancient Ife, a thousand years or more later—who may indeed have learnt the skill from the Nok people.

Nok art is remarkable for the purity of its sculptural

forms, and it may be that there is no other art in the world which better illustrates Cézanne's celebrated dictum urging artists to look in nature for the cylinder, the sphere and the cone. These and other basic forms occur often among the many sculptures which have come to light in the tin-bearing gravels during the past twenty-three years, and one marvels also at the restraint with which decorative detail is always used to enhance the sculptural form rather than for its own sake. The massive head seen in Plate 11, of a man or woman with hands originally clasped on the crown of the head (in a posture characteristic of Badondo woodcarving of the Lower Congo) is the pre-eminent example of the head treated as cylinder; it forms a curious parallel, in the placing of the features as well as the shape, to the Tarascan terracotta figures of western Mexico. The artist of the beautiful head in Plate 12 must surely have been thinking consciously of the form of an egg.

In spite of this great variety in form, certain features such as the pierced triangular eyes are constantly found even when the finds were made as much as 500 kilometres apart. It would seem that two thousand years ago a certain artistic unity existed in a region where it does not exist today. Does this mean that the many tribal styles now found there have been formed by constantly repeated fission and differentiation through the centuries? This is far from certain, and tribal specialization may have existed there as it still does in the Grasslands of Cameroon, an artist of one small tribe executing commissions from chiefs and cults of several other tribes over great distances.

Of all the centres of African art, there is none so remarkable for extraordinary accomplishments in many fields of art as the ancient town of Ife, the ritual centre of the great Yoruba tribe of western Nigeria (and the neighbouring parts of northern Nigeria and of Dahomey). Their terracotta (Plate 13) and bronze (Plates 14 and 15) heads and figures are by far the best-known examples of this talent for the extraordinary. This is idealized naturalism of the most advanced kind. In the midst of African styles so remote from the European tradition, it is indeed extraordinary to find so close a parallel to Greek or Renaissance naturalism, seeming to demand a comparable type and period of evolution to produce it, or else the actual introduction of naturalistic style to Ife from the Mediterranean. Yet a considerable degree of naturalism does occur here and there in African art, and even in the Nok Culture (from which Ife art may be partly or wholly derived); and that this generally latent potentiality in African art should have been developed *à outrance* at Ife becomes less surprising when we consider of what other *tours de main* they were capable. With immense labour they formed and erected slim granite monoliths six metres or more in height; they worked great blocks of quartz (one of the most intractable kinds of stone) into monolithic thrones and other objects of shrine furniture, of immensely complicated forms only to be expected of modellers in a soft medium such as clay; alone of the African peoples they made fully modelled life-size and larger statues in hard stone (just as, in terracotta, they emulated the near life-size figures of the Nok Culture—a feat unequalled by any other African potters); and at the other extreme, there flourished there in mediaeval, pre-European times the greatest glass-bead industry yet brought to light in Africa, now so utterly forgotten that its great fireclay crucibles are interpreted as drums and its waste beads and bead-glass are thought to have grown naturally in the soil. All these distinctions are consistent with the place of Ife in Yoruba myth as the centre and origin of the world. The visitor to the ramshackle and noisome cocoa town of today could have no inkling, save within its museum, of the store which its people once placed on pre-eminence in every field.

The development of the remarkable culture of ancient Ife cannot have been entirely uninfluenced by the elements of Near Eastern culture which were at large in the eastern and western Sudan in the Middle Ages and which so decisively affected the arts of the Akan peoples and of the Nupe and other tribes of northern Nigeria. Yet the Ife style, in the highly developed, sensuously beautiful form seen in Plates 13 to 15, cannot have been transplanted entire from a non-African source, and can best be understood not as a likeness of Greek art but as a unique and aberrant specialization within the more naturalistic end of the African spectrum of forms.

African tribal art is sometimes erroneously described as " folk art " by those who forget that this term is only one-half of a division characteristic of " civilized " societies —the classification of art by social class into " fine art " and " folk art ". It is an essential mark of folk art that it is derived, at a lapse of several decades, from the aristocratic art of the country. This distinguishes folk art from tribal art, which is not stratified and which is indigenous to the tribe. It is often true that tribal chiefs have more sumptuous works of art, richer perhaps in iconographic detail, than the ordinary commoner; but in such cases there is only one style, recognized as that of the tribe as a whole. In fact we may state as a general rule that there is no folk art, properly so-called, in negro Africa; there is, however, one partial exception which may be said to prove the rule, namely the arts of the Benin kingdom.

Benin's great fame as a centre of art derives not from the tribal art of the Bini (which indeed has been unjustly overshadowed) but from the court art of the Oba's palace in Benin City. These are two separate growths, between which there is but little sign of mutual influence. Here, then, we have a clear case of stratified art, corresponding to a stratification in society, yet the tribal art is not derived, except for some latter-day details of subject-matter, from the court art, nor is the court art a specialization or an ennoblement of the tribal art. On the contrary, all the evidence at our disposal tends to confirm the well-established tradition that both the royal dynasty and the court art are of alien origin, having been transplanted from the prestigious Yoruba town of Ife respectively about the thirteenth and fourteenth centuries. It is remarkable that the alien and the indigenous styles should have maintained their separateness to such a degree from the first importation of naturalistic bronze-casting from Ife by the sixth Oba, Oguola, towards A.D. 1400 until well into the nineteenth century (when the Bini chiefs received

Small bronze figure of a warrior, whose free posture is an exceptional departure from the formal rigidity of most African sculpture. Actual size (height of figure: 7.5 cm; total height: 14 cm). Lower Niger Bronze Industry, Federation of Nigeria. (William Fagg Collection. Photo: William Fagg.)

Osemwede's permission to copy his ancestral bronze heads in wood for their own ancestor altars); but this can be accounted for by the rigid controls exercised through the centuries by the absolutist Obas. For instance, it was forbidden to make bronzes except by royal command; the chiefs of the bronze-casters' guild had to be content with terracotta substitutes for their ancestral altars. So it may not be too inappropriate to classify Benin court art as " fine art " (without any implication that it is necessarily better); but we cannot classify the Bini tribal art as " folk art ", in spite of the few " folk " elements derived from the court style in recent times.

The most characteristic works of the court style are the rectangular bronze plaques, of which about a thousand survive and which clad the tall wooden pillars of the Oba's audience chambers. They represent the middle, or classical, period of the bronze art of Benin, from the mid-sixteenth to the mid-seventeenth centuries. Plate 16 shows the Oba enthroned in typically rigid posture between his two supporting chiefs; Plate 17 shows three more chiefs or court officials of similarly impressive stolidity; and Plate 18, the drummer, breaks away from the " academicism " of the first two both in subject-matter and in originality of design, and is in fact by one of a small group of plaque masters whose works are immediately recognizable by their superior artistry.

It seems probable that the rectangular frame was derived through the Portuguese from the pictorial tradition of Europe; but the absence of a " ground line " makes any more specific artistic connection with the Renaissance seem very improbable indeed, even though the Portuguese figure frequently in the iconography of the plaques (Plate 16).

Some of the finest works of the middle period are figures in the round of men and animals (Plate 19). We may say that in general they preserve a recognizable trace of the Ife-like naturalism of the early period; but Plate 20 shows one of two fine female figures, apparently of the period, whose faces are in a radically different and so far un-identified style. Finally, the two centuries of decadence of the late period were relieved from time to time by vigorous, if less harmonious, masterpieces such as the horseman from the north in Plate 21.

By accident of history, the Benin court style is the only African style which can be documented, stage by stage, through four centuries of development. Yet it begins to seem less and less likely that the Ife-Benin succession represents the main stream of bronze-casting art in the Nigerian area. It appears more probable that this stream flows along the lower Niger valley a little to the east of the Benin kingdom, to judge from a group of apparently related bronze-casting styles, provisionally known as the Lower Niger Bronze Industry, of uncertain origin but found at many places on both sides of the river from the delta up to the confluence with the Benue, and, in the case of one important group, as far upstream as Tada and Jebba at the western end of the Nupe country. It is from this group—the Tsoede bronzes—that we illustrate the bowman of Jebba (Plate 22); this figure, its female companion and a third large male figure at Tada are the largest bronze figures so far discovered in negro Africa. The Tsoede group of at least ten bronzes are believed to have been brought to the Nupe country in the fifteenth or early sixteenth century from Idah below the confluence, where they probably formed a single large group on a royal shrine.

All the bronzes of these styles are clearly to be regarded as conceptual rather than imitative works, and the best of them show imaginative qualities of artistic invention which surely surpass anything in the Ife-Benin tradition. Moreover, they may well represent an earlier phase of bronze-casting art, for one important group of bronzes, those excavated at Igbo-Ukwu to the east of the Niger, and remarkable for the rococo-like profusion of their decoration, has recently been dated by carbon-14 testing to the middle of the ninth century.

Plates 23 to 25 reproduce three examples of Yoruba art. The quality which stands out above all in Yoruba sculpture is its humanism, its humanity, the strong tendency of the artists to perform their artistic service to the gods through the natural human form, resorting only very rarely to abstraction, surrealism or expressionism (except in certain masks which are by their nature caricatures). Nowhere else do we find sculpture used for narrative purposes, as on carved doors and other relief sculptures, and this probably arises from the desire of the artists to express the tribal values through homely scenes of daily life. Can we say that this broadly naturalistic character of Yoruba art descends from the much more advanced naturalism of the Ife style of the thirteenth century or thereabouts? It does not seem likely that the sophisticated hierocrats of early Ife could have so leavened the vast mass of the Yoruba; if they had, one would expect that it would have been above all in bronze-casting, yet this is precisely the medium in which the highest degree of abstraction occurs, whereas woodcarving, in which Yoruba naturalism is most prominent, seems to have been of minor importance at ancient Ife. The existence of the Ife style itself, on the other hand, becomes a little easier to understand—whether it was introduced from outside or not—if we suppose that the Yoruba as a whole were already practising a basically naturalistic style of sculpture, which would predispose them as no other African people to accept the sensuously refined modelling of the Ife sculptures as a kind of quintessence of the style that they knew.

The Yoruba are notable, too, for their strong—and undoubtedly ancient—tendency towards urbanism, as an expression of family and clan solidarity. The major religious cults (and therefore the major art forms) are also related to these patterns of settlement, and it would seem entirely natural that a culture which places such emphasis on human relationships should also develop a humanistic art.

Yoruba style preserves a remarkable homogeneity while allowing every locality and village, and even every carver, to develop a distinctive substyle. The unifying elements are due in large part to the great universal cults such as the Ogboni, a cult of the earth spirits which formerly wielded great political power, and the cult of the thunder god, Shango. Plates 23 and 24 show figures in bronze and ivory for the Ogboni. The large bronze figure giving the Ogboni greeting may stand for the male earth spirit and was probably cast in Abeokuta by the Ogundipe family in the nineteenth century; the rare ivory figure of a horseman with Ogboni emblems is an adaptation to the tapering tusk of the style of rather schematic relief carving found on the great drums of the Ogboni. Plate 25 represents a priestess or woman devotee of Shango on a dance staff used in his cult, and beautifully exemplifies the pervading humanism of Yoruba art.

The society and the art of the Ibo (Plate 26) follow a very different direction from those of the Yoruba. Their tendency is towards individualism and the complete avoidance of social stratification (except, in the case of certain title-giving societies, on a basis of wealth, that is to say of individual success). For a tribe of several millions, they have succeeded remarkably through the centuries in preserving their " acephalous " or rulerless way of life, and major towns have arisen only in response to the needs of modern commerce and government. This emphasis on local autonomy extends also to art, and although the Ibo all speak one language, they cannot be said to have one art, as can the Yoruba or their eastern neighbours the Ibibio. They have evolved separate styles as yet uncounted, often changing completely from one village to the next, and lacking any common denominators of style or subject-matter. Indeed, the stylistic variety of forms to be found among the Ibo is almost as great as that of Africa as a whole, ranging from near-naturalism to extreme abstraction. Our example (Plate 26) is from one of the more naturalistic of these styles, and—perhaps significantly—is from Onitsha, the one great commercial entrepôt town founded by the Ibo on the east bank of the Niger, in an area where (as we have seen) kingship has apparently existed in an attenuated form for some eleven centuries. Such white-faced masks are used by the *Mmwo* (spirit) society to propitiate the ghosts of dead women.

These tendencies of the Ibo towards individualism are not present among the Ibibio (Plate 27), and their art is again more homogeneous, although in the area round Ikot Ekpene the range of variation in form, and of artistic invention, is very great, especially in masks. Even at their most abstract, such variations seem to be on a recognizably Ibibio theme. The mask illustrated in Plate 27 is an excellent example of the ability of the old Ibibio carvers to assimilate elements of European subject-matter—in this case an elegant Victorian coiffure which was probably borrowed from European missionary ladies—without loss of style. This mask also exemplifies the common Ibibio practice of carving one or more human or animal heads (or skulls) on the top.

In their language and culture the Ibibio are only distantly related to the Ibo to their north and west, but rather closely to the Ekoi group to the east; in art they have been able to act as a bridge for the passage of influences from east to west, especially through the medium of certain popular dance societies such as the Ekkpe. In particular the naturalistic skin-covered headdresses of the Ekoi have during this century spread first through the related Ibibio where they became so popular that they began to be adopted by the peripheral Ibo, whose existing mask styles, of an entirely different conception, have been progressively displaced. One of the finest of the Ibo styles, that of the *Ogbom* plays of the Bende area, must clearly have been adopted from the neighbouring Ibibio, probably late in the nineteenth century, so closely does it conform to the basic mode of Ibibio sculpture.

In the northern Ekoi country on the Cross River there have been found nearly three hundred stone figures, or rather stone monoliths with human features in low relief, which form one of the few important occurrences of stone-carving art in Africa. It will be seen from Plate 28 that the relief is very shallow, following closely the natural form of the basalt block, and that there is little obvious relationship to woodcarving style. They were still being set up in 1900 as memorials to family heads, and research suggests that they may span a period of three centuries.

With the Ekoi are grouped their neighbours the Boki, the Keaka and the Anyang, on both sides of the Nigeria-Cameroon border; all of these practise the rather realistic style of art represented in the Ekkpe headdress seen in Plate 29, in which a carved wooden head is usually covered

21

with stretched antelope skin to give a lifelike appearance. This realism is, however, often converted into surrealism by the addition of horns, whether actual ones as in this case, or fantastically elaborated and convoluted ones as in many others.

Tribes related to the Ekoi cluster, such as the Bakwiri, the Bakundu and the Bafo, occupy the coastal plains of west Cameroon (and Mount Cameroon) below the escarpment of the Grasslands and as far as the estuary of the Sanaga. Their art, little known except in certain German, Swiss and French collections, is overshadowed by the sculptural riches found above the escarpment, but is by no means without merit.

The sculpture of the Grassland peoples of Cameroon (Plates 30 and 31) is without any doubt the most vigorous to be found in tribal Africa, and at the same time presents some of the most difficult problems in recent art history. The Grasslands, rolling green uplands of volcanic origin and extraordinary beauty, are the home of a large number of small tribes belonging to three main language groups— Tikar, Bamileke and Bamum—which are not closely related; some of the languages of the smaller tribes are understood in only three or four villages. These small tribes or chiefdoms, the main language clusters and the Grassland population as a whole have during the past hundred years been in a most interesting stage of development for students of the dynamics of cultural and artistic change. On the one hand, each chiefdom in which sculpture was practised appears to have had its own distinctive style; on the other hand, the art of the Grasslands as a whole is marked by a number of common tendencies of technique and subject-matter which give it a greater unity than is found in any other large group of tribes in Africa. Between these two levels, the three main language groups each present some tendency to internal stylistic unity, but are not, with our present knowledge, completely separate. It would seem that, however the stylistic differentiation may have occurred, mechanisms have been in operation in recent times which have been promoting greater assimilation between them and perhaps leading towards their assignment to a single great Grasslands style. If evolution had proceeded to that point, we may imagine that the Tikar, Bamileke and Bamum clusters taken together might have presented an aspect rather like that of the Yoruba, who are artistically a unity, even though some large sections of them may have had a different origin from the main body.

Within the broad picture suggested above, a remarkable variety of stylistic problems confronts the fieldworker, and even more the art historian working from published or otherwise recorded information. These peculiar difficulties arise from the highly developed nexus of trading relationships between the numerous tribes, and, no doubt, from its distortion in successive changes of sovereignty—from tribal independence through German, British, French and Nigerian administration to national independence. Many small tribes specialize in particular forms of artistic production such as brass-casting, the making of richly ornamented pottery tobacco pipes (which are carved rather than modelled), weaving and embroidery, and in particular woodcarving. Although every tribe undoubtedly had some carvers of its own, a number of tribes were so famous for finely carved thrones, figures, masks, bowls, drums or houseposts that their works are, or were, found in most villages over very wide areas; owners are most commonly able to state, if asked, the origin of their pieces, and a comprehensive expedition to study stylistic distribution, mutual influences, etc., is urgently needed before both objects and information disappear.

It may well be that rivalries arising from this situation have encouraged the bold originality and vigorous sense of movement for which Grasslands art is pre-eminent. Our examples well illustrate these qualities. Plate 30 represents a mask in the style of Wum in the north-western Grasslands, of the same cubist-expressionist type as a mask in the late Tristan Tzara's collection which directly inspired one of Picasso's finest bronzes. Plate 31 is a detail from one of the great beaded thrones in the palace at Banjun in south-eastern Bamileke, and shows a strong affinity with the spirally conceived movement of the finest Bangwa figures.

We shall continue our journey to survey African sculpture in the parallel volume *The Art of Central Africa*, where we examine the sculptural styles found beyond the Sanaga River. For the moment, however, we shall conclude our artistic grand tour of the vast area geographically unified by the Niger river system and examined in the present volume with the art of the ancient culture of Lake Chad (Plate 32), the so-called Sao Culture (though Sao does not appear to have been a name used by its members). This important group, whose principal modern descendants are the Kotoko tribe, is believed by its French discoverers to have flourished from about the sixth to the seventeenth centuries, but most of the terracotta sculptures (such as our figure) and the decorative bronzes are thought to date from the later part of this period. The culture seems to have first been identified in some little-known excavations in Nigeria, but of the works of art nearly all have been discovered, so far, in Cameroon and Chad. Sao terracottas bear little obvious resemblance to those of any other part of Africa, and in particular do not seem to be related to the Nok Culture which flourished at an earlier time about 800 kilometres to the south-west; the forms of Nok sculpture appear more strongly structured and schematic, while those of the Sao, though very characteristic and distinctive, exhibit a less well-defined kind of abstraction. The importance which the Nok art may well have had in the early development of Nigerian art history does not so far seem to be paralleled for Sao art, though we should possibly take account of recent pottery sculpture of the Waja, Longuda and other upper Benue tribes which may have been influenced by it. Yet who knows what, but for the climate and the termites, their wood sculpture might have shown?

ILLUSTRATIONS

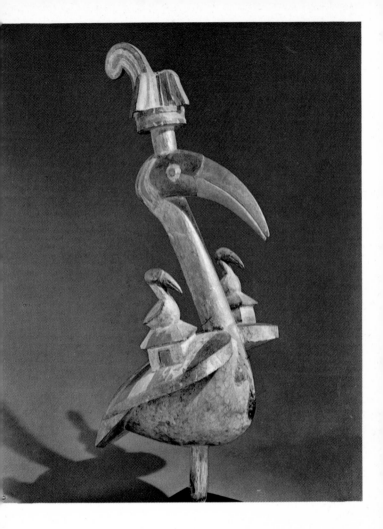

2

3

4

12

14

16

18

19

24

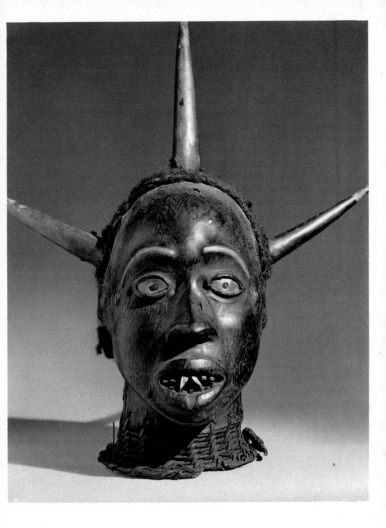

CONTENTS

The colour photographs for this volume were specially taken by Mario Carrieri.

CONTENTS

Continued overleaf ▶

CONTENTS

BIBLIOGRAPHY

DELANGE, J.; LEIRIS, M., *L'art nègre*, Paris, Gallimard, 1967 (L'univers des formes).

FAGG, William, *Nigerian images*, New York, Praeger; London, Lund Humphries, 1963.

FAGG, William; PLASS, Margaret, *African sculpture: an anthology*, New York, Dutton; London, Studio Vista, 1964.

FAGG, William, *Tribes and forms in African art*, New York, Tudor, 1965; London, Methuen, 1966.

FAGG, William, *African tribal sculptures*, 2 vols., London, Methuen, 1966.

GOLDWATER, Robert, *Bambara sculpture from the western Sudan*, New York, Museum of Primitive Art, 1960

GOLDWATER, Robert, *Senufo sculpture from West Africa*, New York, Museum of Primitive Art, 1964.

LAUDE, Jean, *Les arts de l'Afrique noire*, Paris, Livre de poche, 1966.

LECOQ, Raymond, *Les Bamiléké*, Paris, Editions africaines, 1953 (Présence africaine).

LEUZINGER, Elsy, *Africa: the art of the negro peoples*, New York, McGraw-Hill; London, Methuen, 1960 (Art of the world).

TROWELL, Margaret, *Classical African sculpture*, London, Faber, 1964.

UNDERWOOD, Leon, *Bronzes of West Africa*, London, Tiranti, 1949.

UNDERWOOD, Leon, *Figures in wood of West Africa; statuettes en bois de l'Afrique occidentale*, London, Tiranti, 1964.

UNDERWOOD, Leon, *Masks of West Africa; masques de l'Afrique occidentale*, London, Tiranti, 1964.

Printed in Italy